Math Counts

Capacity

Children's Press®

An Imprint of Scholastic Inc.

About This Series

In keeping with the major goals of the National Council of Teachers of Mathematics, children will become mathematical problem solvers, learn to communicate mathematically, and learn to reason mathematically by using the series Math Counts.

Pattern, Shape, and *Size* may be investigated first—in any sequence.

Sorting, Counting, and *Numbers* may be used next, followed by *Time, Length, Weight,* and *Capacity.*

—*Ramona G. Choos, Professor of Mathematics,*
Senior Adviser to the Dean of Continuing Education, Chicago State University;
Sponsor for Chicago Elementary Teachers' Mathematics Club

Author's Note

Mathematics is a part of a child's world. It is not only interpreting numbers or mastering tricks of addition or multiplication. Mathematics is about ideas. These ideas have been developed to explain particular qualities such as size, weight, and height, as well as relationships and comparisons. Yet all too often the important part that an understanding of mathematics will play in a child's development is forgotten or ignored.

Most adults can solve simple mathematical tasks without the need for counters, beads, or fingers. Young children find such abstractions almost impossible to master. They need to see, talk, touch, and experiment.

The photographs and text in these books have been chosen to encourage talk about topics that are essentially mathematical. By talking, the young reader can explore some of the central concepts that support mathematics. It is on an understanding of these concepts that a student's future mastery of mathematics will be built.

—*Henry Pluckrose*

Math Counts

Capacity

By Henry Pluckrose

Mathematics Consultant: Ramona G. Choos, Professor of Mathematics

Children's Press®

An Imprint of Scholastic Inc.

Have you ever played with damp sand,
packed it into a pail,

and made a sandcastle? Why does the sand take the shape of the pail?

A water bottle, a jar, a thimble,
a cup, and a pail are all containers.
Containers hold things.
Inside a container there is a space.

The space inside a container can hold solids, liquids, or just air.

Here are some containers.
If you filled each of them with water,

can you guess which would hold the most and which would hold the least?

It is sometimes easy to guess which container will hold the most water when they are different sizes.

It is much more difficult to guess
when the containers look almost the same.

Guessing can be difficult.
Which of these two containers
holds the most?
We must measure to find out.

Pour water from the pitcher into the dish. What does this tell you?

Now collect some empty containers.
How can you tell
which one will hold the most water
and which one will hold the least?

We do not have to use water.
We could use sand or marbles instead.
The sand fills all the space in the glass.
Do the marbles fill all the space?

Often we need to measure exactly.
We may use fluid ounces, quarts, and gallons
as standard measures for liquids.
Or we may use liters and milliliters.
Many drinks are sold both ways

and so are many other things.

A quart is quite a large measure.
Smaller quantities are measured in cups, and fluid ounces
A liter is quite a large measure also.
Smaller quantities are measured in deciliters or milliliters.

4.2 FL OZ ℮ 125 ml

There are eight fluid ounces in a cup.

There are four cups in a quart.

There are ten deciliters in a liter.

There are a thousand milliliters in a liter.

Standard measures are important. The ingredients for a cake have to be mixed in the right quantities.

1CUP 8OZ 1CUP
3/4 6 2/3
1/2 4 1/3
1/4 2

Garden fertilizers have to be carefully measured.

Medicines must be measured carefully when they are made

and when we take them.

Standard measures help us to measure exactly. When a driver buys a gallon, or a liter, of gasoline, she knows exactly how much she will get wherever she buys it.

The gasoline runs from the pump into the car's gas tank. When the tank is full, it will hold no more gas. *Capacity* is the word used to describe the most that a container can hold.

Some containers are very large.
This tanker holds many gallons, or liters.

These drums hold chemicals.
Which container has the greater capacity,
a tanker or a drum?

Being able to measure capacity is important. What might happen to this ship if too much coal was loaded onto it?

What might happen to this reservoir if too much water went into it?

Capacity is not the same as weight.
The pasta fills the jar and so does the water.
Which do you think is heavier?

Capacity is a word we use to describe space, even when the space is empty.

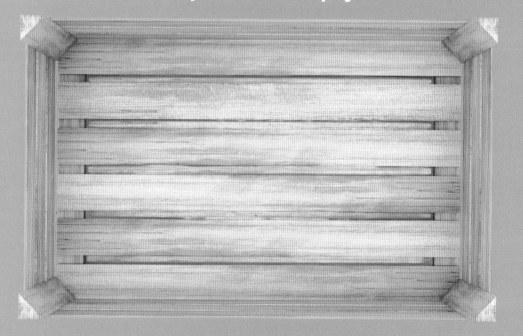

Index

Reader's Guide

Visit this Scholastic Web site to download the Reader's Guide for this series:
www.factsfornow.scholastic.com Enter the keywords **Math Counts**

Library of Congress Cataloging-in-Publication Data
Names: Pluckrose, Henry, 1931- author. | Choos, Ramona G., consultant.
Title: Capacity/by Henry Pluckrose; mathematics consultant: Ramona G. Choos, Professor of Mathematics.
Other titles: Math counts.
Description: Updated edition. | New York, NY: Children's Press, an imprint of Scholastic Inc., [2018] | Series: Math counts | Includes index.
Identifiers: LCCN 2017061283| ISBN 9780531175064 (library binding) | ISBN 9780531135150 (pbk.)
Subjects: LCSH: Volume (Cubic content)—Juvenile literature. | Weights and measures—Juvenile literature.
Classification: LCC QC104 .P58 2018 | DDC 530.8—dc23
LC record available at https://lccn.loc.gov/2017061283

Copyright © The Watts Publishing Group, 2018
Printed in Heshan, China 62

Scholastic Inc., 557 Broadway, New York, NY 10012.

Credits: Photos ©: cover: sellingpix/iStockphoto; 1: sellingpix/iStockphoto; 3: sellingpix/iStockphoto; 4: Brian Pieters/Getty Images; 5: Nine OK/Getty Images; 6-7, 11, 12-13, 30 table: nuwatphot/Shutterstock; 6 pail: DenisNata/Shutterstock; 6 cup: Svitlana-ua/Shutterstock; 8-9, 14 table: kibri_ho/Shutterstock; 10, 15, 18 table: donatas1205/Shutterstock; 20: Mark Deibert Productions/Shutterstock; 21: Phanie/Alamy Stock Photo; 22: Erik Isakson/Getty Images; 23: De Agostini Picture Library/Getty Images; 24: MOHAMED EL-SHAHED/AFP/Getty Images; 25: Justin Sullivan/Getty Images; 26: macroworld/iStockphoto; 27: vchal/iStockphoto; 28: Ade lukmanul hakimm/Shutterstock; 29: Filippo Manaresi/Getty Images; 31 top: JoKMedia/iStockphoto; 31 bottom: gorica/iStockphoto.

All other images © Bianca Alexis Photography.